Prima Materia

Thom Boulton

WATERHARE
PRESS

PRIMA MATERIA
A WATERHARE PRESS BOOK
ISBN: 978-1-9993112-2-3

Text copyright © Thom Boulton 2018

Cover Artwork copyright © Clare Boulton 2018
with thanks to Chris Uren

First Edition: 23 November 2018
Edited by Sara Elizabeth Smiles

The artwork featured in the Waterhare Press logo
is copyright © Pam Richards 2018

Waterhare Press is based in Plymouth, UK
waterharepress@publicist.com

Contents

Fermented Truths

A Side Of Sublimation

Coagulated Oil

With thanks to

Julian Isaacs

Benjamin Serpell

Sara Elizabeth Smiles

for their critical eyes.

With thanks to

Matthew Carbery

Dan Morgan

Kenny Knight

William Telford

Steve Spence

Simon Travers

for their encouragement.

for C.G.B, P.R.B, and G.E.B.

Preface

Prima Materia is a primordial substance and completely formless. It is the beginning of the magnum opus (the great work) which leads to the philosopher's stone. With intention, the alchemist can manipulate the quintessence into something incredible. Transformation is an art and with it our minds can act as a tesseract, expanding and growing exponentially. If our brain is the universe waiting to be born, then thought is the explosion which brings it into being.

It is the magician's want to follow the steps of transformation on their terms however this does not always happen; sometimes great change comes about naturally or by force. At the age of eighteen, I was diagnosed with clinical depression. The doctor informed me that despite coming to terms with the events that had pushed me into the abyss, my brain was refusing to let me escape. I was prescribed medication and that was that. The medication was helpful and allowed me to function to some degree, however more events and circumstances pressed down upon me and my inner anger and hatred of myself grew fierce. These thoughts plagued me and erupted in noticeable ways. This was not a cry for help but a yell, a scream to those around me that if this continued I couldn't tell where it would take me.

Thankfully it was noticed and I began reclaiming my life back from the clutches of the black dragon. At this stage I was 'prima materia', completely formless, but thanks to meeting an incredible person and falling romantically in love with her, I started to take shape. The process of transformation continued over the years and eventually led me to Druidry. For the first time in my life I understood myself, why I thought the way I did; why I felt the way I did, and that I wasn't the only soul out there who felt out of place in the world. The love I received from my wife and the acceptance I gained from becoming part of the pagan community, helped me find a place where I felt strong again.

Yet it wasn't until I became a father for the first time that I realised what I needed more than strength, was weakness. To be weak and not break is something that fatherhood forced me to experience. It taught me that I could fear so many things yet still stay strong for my children. This collection of poetry explores the events, feelings, and personal experiences which took place between 2005 and 2018. The works cover a wide range of subject matters including; mental health, toxic relationships, death, bereavement, love, romance, religion, spirituality, breaking paradigms, paganism, politics, fatherhood, the future, education, climate change, the environment, robotics, the occult, culture, David Bowie (I'm still not over it), friendship, society, people, gender, and probably some other stuff as well...

I have been very fortunate to have some of the pieces in this book published prior to this first edition of Prima Materia.

She, *first published in The Broadsheet, 2017*

Smell a Rat, *first published on Strange-Poetry.com, 2017*

Dragonfly, *first published in The Dawntreader, 2018*

Expanding Universe, *first published on uglywriters.com, 2018*

The Song Didn't Play, *first published in Domestic Cherry, 2018*

23:23, *to be published by Epizootics, 2018/19*

A Short While Later, *to be published by Epizootics, 2018/19*

My thanks to those who took a chance on me and shared my poetry with their readers.

Actuality

Upon croaky timbers rests the actor's feet
tired from walking lines, taking directions
on the face is a simmering bead of sweat
its membership revoked, it slides stilly o'er

brow, tidying up things before decamping
time escapes the ticking metal hands, thick
brushes sweep the dot from the Universe
now it is dead, an unaccomplished descent

no great body of works etched on forehead
a paupers grave for the blob, never a trace
when it sleeps in the void it does not dream
nor scream, for some miracles do befall us.

Leaky Taps

Calcination: The destruction of the ego. The self crumbles away either deliberately (in alchemy) or unhealthily due to afflictions and experiences.

Bathroom Floor

The bath mat is
sodden, soaked
by an overflow of
dirty bath water.

Shivering bristles
shake off pneumonia
by taking a dose
of ibuprofen
baptised in whisky.

Matted material
conjures an image
of a drowning seabird,
a thick-billed murre
or maybe a brown noddy,
fished out by a
conservationist.

The bird does not feel rescued.

Over time, mildew
erupts like a rash,
pox marks cause a
sunken appearance
in the fabric, no tub
filled with oats
will ever help it recover.
The bath mat still
has its uses
allowing soaked toes

to step over it
but this merely adds
moisture, causes more
mould.

Black holes.

A deteriorated form
sucking in
all the light.
If it wanted to be seen
it would leave its own
footprint, a digital dent
so when people
googled it there'd be
some sort of presence.

But for now
it's happy to
take a page
out of Simon's songbook
and enjoy
the cold silence

disrupted
occasionally

by the dripping of
leaky taps.

Our Thoughts Are With The Family At This Time.

There was a plate of food
minding its own business

and a pint glass casually
studying text messages,

neither of them expected
to see a newspaper unfold,

black ink from the headline
coursing down both cheeks,

there was no need to read
the byline resting on his brow,

she meant something to him,
a crush of long hair one summer
suffocated his heart, her heart
stopped.

a picture of a phoenix on the wall,
didn't dare to come off the page,

he wondered how anyone could
smile after that, teeth were chalk

and dried the throat like ice,
no chance to speak or mutter,

she'd taught him to talk on the phone,
demonstrated her yoga positions,

he was unsure if this time, maybe,
she hadn't recovered from a position,

lost in a triangle or downward dog.

Mender

Neon bulbs popping like blister packs.

He came rising from the chair, a balloon made of quartz,
the other people kept still but noticed him ghosting,

no third eye needed to spy his spirit
pulling his childish, stubborn hand.

Collapsing down - he spoke in tongues,
deflated the room with anecdotes,
photo frames fell off the walls with a quiver of his lip,

he'd never seen a doctor cry before,
all it took was a statement.

The Drowned God

A mop of seaweed
clung
vehemently to the scalp.

The corner of the mouth
lay home to caviar - no
biscuits, freshly laid.

The skin of a beluga,
baptised every day
for a week until
weak pigment remained.

Nails hard as barnacles.
Barnacles don't grow
they simply
look larger when the
tide is out. Crescent moon
shows.

A lone starfish covered
by seabed dirt,
it's what happens when
relaxed, apparently.
Concave palms cupped,
placed to the ear
one can hear sounds of
the ocean; the struggle.

No wallet to identify.

Noughts and Crosses

We sat with crossed legs
and nought to do. Broke
flesh with a pen to carve
a hatched board, you told
me you wouldn't win, I
agreed. Marked with no
eraser to undo. It was
painless to lose until the
sting of metal teeth cut
deeper. Everything fades.
Memories pour out one
ear, skin forgets a summer
tan, and old childhood
games become misplaced.

To Be Put To Death By Needles

Lobotomised with a chewed biro.

Quartered with a burnt sausage.

Snapped like a crisp, dry cracker.

Hugged tightly by a soft smile.

Beaten with pennies in a striped sock.

Rodded by the cord of a g-string.

Gifted a sweet kiss inside a locket.

Scolded with a junior thesaurus.

Garrotted by a heartfelt letter.

Healed by two thumbs waltzing.

Screwed by the hinge of semantics.

Asphyxiated by a pirate copy of a DVD.

Unsound Reality

Dissolution: Drowning in a less rational world. Dreams and feelings flood us and reveal a world that feels different to our desires.

Dragonfly

Yesterday was fond of tomorrow
but they had never met, sang to each

other on strange astral planes made of
never written songs, unsent birthday

cards, and red marks left from pinches. The
river and the riverbed are kin,

brother and sister. In the river-
bed, mud is thicker than water, the

dragonflies dance around reeds and speak
the incantation of could / would / might,

they wait for the previous day to
become the next but they know deep down

in their thorax that it will never
present. A nymph not shed. Instead, they

dream up a universal quantum
field capable of transferring form

over certain parameters, a
transformation, they believe it will

mean, in some reality, a multi-
verse or stream of possibilities,

dusk knows morning, they have sat by the
river watching dragonflies cast spells

in the witching hour, the last day has
met the next. Embryonic sunrise.

Vesuvius

Heart felt like a volcano shelled
by endless gunners testing artillery.

Vesuvius erupted in 1944.

Your cold face was dormant,
arms placed over your chest,
a sleepy giant so small, you lay
hushed like the stillness of
a Tibetan monk.

Vesuvius did not erupt in 2007
although it wanted to,
'asleep for now' it said on the
September issue of
National Geographic.

You died in June five months after her.

- - -

She used to feed me cabbage cores,
tough clump of root gnawed away
until nothing remained.

Vacant stares littered the corridor
occasionally met by lucid arms and
desperate fingers, gnawing away
until the clasp relinquished.

You died five months before him.

No goodbye.

In a dream you sang a lullaby,
I needed a pencil to jot down
the tone of your voice,
but I've never drawn a treble clef correctly,
the fear of losing the tune
made my brain melt to a puddle of piss.

I imagine it to be a similar feeling
to what is felt when a volcano is shelled
by endless gunners testing artillery.

- - -

The story of streets on fire
from the bombs, riding bikes
amongst embers of attrition
was only learnt after the end.

She died in 2012 from a hug.

In the moments I held her,
she saw him standing near me,
I'd never met his face but knew it well
from trapped memories in frames,
paused moments.

There was a warmth.
The dry chamber
of my heart replaced by fairy lights,
closed within a box
and stored in the attic.

When saying goodbye to
the turkey and tinsel, there is
a closure of the holiday period,
a sense of acceptance that
Christmas
has finally come to its end.

Excitement seems out of reach
for at least 364 days,
but midwinter signals midsummer,
the gifts of the hollow hill
bring comfort.

At Home With Judas

Cotton ball stuffed into the lung
like a grandmother's hand violating a turkey,
and you there – eating it all up,

hiding in the grasses of thick black hair,
carved a strip with the lawnmower
one Saturday morning,
the neighbours joined in
shaving their gardens in the sun,
and you were there – soaking it all up,

she was so sad
when the pears dropped,
made a fresh juice
that did not quench
but there was you – drinking it all in,

the magazines and papers,
Sunday morning perusal,
articles with shady pictures
and text as bold as a barefaced lie
told to close friends,
and there was you, reading our faces,
forcing yours with an iron will,
steam pressed straight – not a crease.

Eidetic

On the windowsill
sits the statuette of a black dragon
wilfully frozen,
passing time by
watching condensation race

down the clear pane of reality.
It refuses to move
having grown accustom to
taking up the x and y axis
of this particular portion of space,

not one minute passes where
the owner of the statuette
doesn't try to move it.
Hands fail, instead an attempt
is made to dissolve the object,

force it to phase out of time and
become lost amongst the
missing socks and
vanished trinkets
so often wandering the continuum

rather than being where they should be.
With eyes squinting and
straining to the point that
pupils get the bends, thought
manifests to erase each atom,

dissipate every facet of the black dragon
until it resembles the owner's feelings.
Too long has a sense of detachment
haunted, a blur amongst painted faces,
Seurat's pointillism allows for

distilling the dots that make the world,
the gaps (although finite) are large,
large enough to crowbar apart – set adrift
and unmake formed shapes.
Yet the black dragon refuses to obey.

Dust has fallen into dunes
upon the windowsill and now
the statuette reminds the owner
of a time when feet were pressed in sand,
and the stranger looked hard enough,

long enough, to stop movement.
The 'What Ifs?' nod towards an alternate reality,
one where the black dragon forced
an evacuation of the entire living room,
leaving a damp pizza box as a tombstone.

Deciphered Key

Separation: A physical/psychological renewal. The best part of us is revealed and a new energy emerges.

Love Speaks Not With Words

Sat in Sophie's,
two diners,
no utterance,
no muttered words,
a dormant state
as they waited
between
late morning wake up
and the two sausages on a grill
hoping to make it into
their All Day Breakfasts.

She, turned all the mayonnaise packets
to face him.

He, ordered the ketchup packets
to advert their gaze.

A condiment chess-board,
where neither nerd
was aware
of what
they were doing.

More Reversi and less bishop to queen,
he correcting her turns,
she unpicking his.

In that instance
time stood calm,
unable to comment on them.

The tablecloth gawped,
impressed at the pace
of their natural silence.

The salt shaker was a filled vial
of medieval monkhood,
the glass jar of flowers a
collection of
'love-in-idleness',
but they had no need for such things.

Drunk on each other,
intoxicated by their spinning of
salad cream packets
and HP sachets.

Love speaks not with words
but in shared quietude.

Pissing on the Lamppost

Two cats lapping from a dish, one eye
scratched and the other one clawed,
both pissed on the lamppost and

rusted the exoskeleton of an otherwise
stable luminescent pillar, pacing across
paved slabs, tripped on the sticky out

edge and yowled at the stars, walking
stealthily until shadow spooked and
ruptured feet into a defensive bolt, quicker

than a needle jab but the scruff needed
yanking to get in that cage, get in that
cage and go to the vets. Weeping whiskers

like week old flowers, *sorrys* caught in
matted fur balls, lodged on prickly tongue
and refusing to move, eventually the

daytime stole attention and forced two
cats to sleep, lounging on *I love yous*, all
was forgiven and the startled tails sunk.

**Contemplating the Vastness of a
Spackled Ceiling Whilst Listening to
The BeeGees in Bed.**

The BeeGees playlist continues
to play, shuffle button ensures
a pleasant mix of tracks to make
love to, making groovy love to
New York Mining Disaster 1941,
oh yes, oh yeah.

The tea-lights expired, only
a clear puddle remains,
both depleted vessels
long to cuddle the flame,
gentle, gently, rest poor wick,
you've done well.

The creatures both stare at
the ceiling, they gaze lovingly,
the spackled ceiling,
she contemplates their closeness,
his arm is uncomfortable and
she's extremely hot now,
he ponders philosophically over
why you would put sawdust
in paint and apply it as decoration.

The track finishes and romance
vibrates upon the speakers, woofer.

How Deep Is Your Love?

She yearns to sing it to him,
she is unaware that from
all the huffing and sloppy kisses,
her throat has
abandoned impressing him,
it now seals a film upon
the back of her tonsils,
forces her voice to sound like
Kermit the Frog stoned.

He laughs at her funny voice,
a string of snot
escapes his
nasal cavity curious
as to what all the laughing is about.
She gags. She urges.
Phlegm is not her thing.

They begin to reminisce about
the kebab box in the front room.
They wonder what it is up to now,
how far has it come as a person,
has it learnt to walk because they
have now forgotten? They want
sustenance. He jokes about
Salad Cream, she muffles about
a microwave. They check the doorway
but God is real; evolution stinks,
there is no sign
the meat has grown legs.
After bartering, one of them
slips out of the bed's skin,
heads towards feeding tube,

suddenly realises she is nude
and eyes from next door are
examining her from pits down.

She freezes. Phryne. Venus.
Goddess gazing.
A crown of holly for the
crown chakra, peeking acorns
awake in a heat wave.

Embarrassment is a
flattering shade all over.

Hurriedly she escapes
to the lounge, grabs
the kebab and returns,
clutching it to conceal
the spiral dance she
does to jump into bed.

After eating they sleep.
After sleeping they eat.

Everything is static,
time infinite; space
much like a
spackled ceiling.

Naked

When I stripped my clothes off
they became possessed – not air.
A figure formed, the buttons
eyed me and passed judgment.
Milky blues squinted to decide
fate. Could my hair be unravelled
as a cotton wheel, loose from my
mother's wicker basket? The
sleeves went flat to break my back,
slammed, ordered community
service. They made a teacher out
of me by dyeing pound coins red
and slapping me in the face with
a fake, rolled up degree. Congrat-
ulations Mrs Boulton, it's a civil
servant. The stitching in the shin
of my jeans read through my CV,
made suggestions and labelled
my measurements with bullet
points – sharp as poppers on a fly.
I tried but the wigs and whips
broke flesh, lacerated until steam
escaped and faded my body.
Hard times breaking rocks with
your skull – repeating the same
questions with only doubt ever
bothering to reply. If God were real
I imagine him to be sat on the toilet
crushing silver fish under his shoes.
When I stripped bare I saw marks
on my arms, old scars and contours

I was unfamiliar with. For the first
time I knew how many chest hairs
I had, I knew their names; met all
of their kids. I scolded the material,
this time I was judge. Being naked,
you feel the cold more, squirm
at heat, you know what pigment
is hiding beneath, how different
it is to the colouring and freckles
others see.

The Philosopher's Child

Conjunction: The creation of a new person. A new belief system in need of nurturing to survive. Fragile. A hermaphrodite of both worlds.

Night in the Valley

Moonset
a shadow hugs the sky

the stars are not shy
but still

coyly they stretch
to lure faces

tilt upwards

praying to a god or saint
speaking old names
but using pseudonyms

the stride of a cat startles
its legs shuffle as it drifts
a tide of fur
crashing into hedgerows
from left to right

it was formerly a wise man
and offers a blessing

moving forward through a track
six hands make a sign
shaking fingers nearly dislocate

the cat once again strides
between an elderflower and
a clump of dancing dandelions
they sway due to the feline
rubbing itself against them

after it has called it allows movement
once again

six pupils strain in the black
a shape spirals
coiled to engulf and suffocate

venomous snake from a basket

weaving in a midnight heat
conjuring anxiety to manifest
as three young boys

clung to charms
the cat abandons its walk

it will not enter further
neither will their bodies
they struggle to drag six feet forward

but they do

in amongst nightmares of trees
leaning over to grab and claw

in amongst rustling figures
escaping overgrown binding

in amongst the creeping hairs
wrestling free from pores
they see a face

on the other side
neither one speaks
three voices lost

once hidden from the valley
at the break
three hands draw

That Date

Cold concrete chilling the arse cheeks, and
embers lighting the dark for pedestrians, a
lonely step in the wrong direction – but safe.

Still chilled but now the space acts as foreplay,
touching leggings and touching tongues, it
is the birth of a dynasty in a drunken language.

This time a tune escapes the tree line and sails
past residences, it holds a name in its hands,
it is his – calling, he sees a piper is the source.

When returning, he found dust and rubble,
a substitute for the crumbled mess he once
breathed in, the tree line now hidden by brick.

The Cult

a lifeless dressing gown
hung on a hanger

and a thread sprung out
like a broken metal mattress

and someone opening a window
on a cold day

all forced my naked body to
reconsider how it stood
when looking in the mirror

the follicles all grew self-conscious
with every bitter breath spat across them

someone suggested
they'd feel more comfortable
sat down and hidden
by a stone pillar
penetrating a pew

the girth was intimidating
to my naked frame
and forced my body's hands
to be defensive
organising themselves
to cover the good bits
leaving all the scars in the open

the vultures circled

an orbit of the pulpit

shrill cries sounded like being a child
and falling in line with a ringing bell
ready to listen and learn and ingest dictated ideas
a cup sat on a table
and whispered poison
to anyone who took a sip from it

a prison guard offered
a biscuit for nourishment
but only filled my belly with questions

wearing the dressing gown
did nothing for my figure
and boredom caught itself
around the thread
unpicking slowly
with every turning digit

they shut the window
when the weather got hot
a bastard sweat lodge
forcing hallucinations
to intoxicate my mind
and drown the void
charged with carrying
all the thoughts around

bruises appeared on the brain
a sign of abuse

crosses marked where to inflict

the next dose

The Leader and The Leader's Ideas

the whole place smelt like
pickled eggs in paper bags

at some point
I'm not sure when
a rescue operation
bashed down the doors
and shined torch lights
in my body's eyes

pupils constricted
adjusted

it took time to rehabilitate all the blemishes
a 30 degree wash wasn't strong enough

it needed 180 degrees
of pure fire
to set the dressing gown ablaze

the flames reached higher
than English oak trees
and rode like waves
across a winsome sky
summoning rains
with each puff of grey smoke
until all that remained in the clearing
was my bare skeleton

Reading bones instead of books
and books instead of instruction manuals

my mind checked into rehab
and made love to my soul once again

the press gathered
to ask about my escape
but they couldn't hear my voice as it sang

they were busy being deafened by the bells

too caught up in getting themselves ready
to listen and learn and ingest dictated ideas

and I was preoccupied anyway
rolling around the fresh soil
getting grass stains tattooed
onto the surface of each of my bones

Creature to the Witch

And might she spy a wolf dressed in brown fur
she would take an inch of its roughness
lock it away in a silver sterling chain
and claim it fed her confidence

a brittle figure made tough
like water when it burns into steam

the liver fetched from the beast
could cleanse deeper than a smudge

chasing leaves
panting wildly

a heart beat
taming howls

jagged eyes
an arcane sword

the mystic

Baphomet

In front was a painting

the inability to see it
came from a thick layer
of grease smudged
across the eyes

the blurriness of the image
caused the subject to
feel fear

were the rock to have eyes
and a mouth to yell
they would warn
(as they were thrown)
that the unknown
was nothing more
than a familiar tune
unheard for a long time

a distant star whose light
has taken billions of years
to reach the retina
of a stargazer

patience became dry
and cracked

the lust to peek
consumed

with every scrape
the grease fell
congealing angrily
on the subjects shoes
pulling feet back
a child in tantrum

eyes freed themselves
and the painting
stripped bare

the gazing between them
strong enough to lift a brick
or stack stones
into crooked architecture

they noticed each other

two stars exchanging looks
and glances

no artistry to be bound

Gigantomachy

a man of renown

the skull as large as the ego

when the Titans ruled

earth-born

intangible

should legs be serpents

and an apple held to the sky

the great flood sent to soak

the disembodied spirit

gills shaped like three staves

Gaia's womb stirs

a revolution; an instance

shadows of the scholar

understood

The Book of Days

When the otherworld lay up
    sweat fell like a waterfall
    and cracks leaked shadows

When the young tors opened up
    gulped the indent of footprints
    and learnt to dance themselves

When sycamore discovered
    it was an acorn and not
    a winged seed spiralling

When Manwydden drifted free
    seeking a cauldron to brew
    healing scars of the dead

When the Hanging Stones stood
    demanding the mind to form
    vibrating harmony

When Orion was just a man
    not yet learning he was both
    hunter and Cailleach

When the Horned God sang his tune
    stepped on dirt to make the green
    a father to the woods

When a name was bitten/chewed
    and kept deep in a stomach
    digested by the old

Fermented Truths

Fermentation: The need to express new meaningful images/thoughts. The muses have come to visit and inspire a new channel between the mind (the real world) and the soul (the spiritual world).

She

Last night I walked home in the darkness
but the darkness wasn't there.

She was sort of vacant
and not really talkative.
I think she'd shifted her shape,
some sort of indiscernible moon phase
or something
and
although she wasn't obvious,
I could still feel her hair
flicking on my face, a whip
across the eyes,
her attempt at flirting.

When we got to the door,
I leaned in for a
goodnight kiss but
I just kind of stood there, alone,
waiting
but never really
contemplating
how much of a goon I looked, pursed lips
protruding in the darkness
with no return or
mutual feelings acknowledged.

I'm not sure where she was,
probably out
doing something important
like

spooking some kids
walking home or
poking her head up
in a Fleetwood Mac song.

I stopped with the lip motion and
headed up to my front door
alone.

Funny thing was though
when I got to the top step I realised
the door wasn't there either.

Goodbye Catherine Munroe

A biscuit made of wit, crumbles,
becomes soggy. Dunked
into a brewing cup of defensive comments.
Fingers pinch hold of the last bit. Pangea
has broken apart –

all that is left are masses
floating in a chaotic drink.

At the time
it seemed a good idea.
Tea stains white shirts.
You can't make a flag and
wave it if stained by
misspoken words. Timing

is everything. Kettles pop
to let you know they're ready.

He had the timing of a saucepan of milk.

Guesswork.

A pungent smelling skin forms.
Apologies come in three sizes,
different depending on the mug.

Scribed names
upon the side of a paper cup are
helpful, when done drinking
it can be used for begging.

The name gives ownership. When he
apologised to Catherine, he did it at Costa. Cost him
a fortune in dry cleaning when she gave her reply.

A quick flick and
twenty years of
'not-good-enoughs'
spilled out
across his
freshly dry-cleaned shirt.

She keyed the word knob into his tie using a Chai Latte.

He'd torn the Canderel packet
that was her heart,
one too many times.

The crowd scolded him with
blistering looks, the third degree.
No one gave a shit if he'd been burnt.

They knew he'd been burned.

Fambles

Two hands walked side by side,
holding pride deep inside knuckles,
buried so the eyes could not judge distance
or proximity
to be anything more than
a lower orbit of two celestial objects.
The ears felt like pricks,
heard old sayings which caused wax to block,
a few drops of permissive oil
lubricated ideals to dislodge.
The two hands ruptured in bruises,
broken blood vessels from the pressure of
repression.
The contusion contrasted with other marks,
a spectrum of red to yellow, to
blue and purple,
a skin graft of scales from Boeseman's fish,
a sense of freedom
displayed with dignity.

Smell a Rat

In confined spaces
you can
really get
a good whiff,
really smell
someone's neck,
something you don't often
get a chance to do
in normal
circumstances.

If there were such a thing as
Halal buses, or Kosher,
they could say a prayer or
blessing
before everyone's packed
into the killing floor.

What is this need to cram? To overcrowd?

Put a smeared cotton bud,
swabbed with a bead of sweat,
under the microscopic lens of a microcosm
and watch the population boom.

What's next?

Will the buses be
stuffed in
bigger buses?

£16.95 for a
bird within a bird
within a bird,
within a bird, within a bird
within a bird.
Six bird roast is what his neck smelt like.
Six bird roast is what his neck looked like.

Cut a slither and serve with
a gravy made
from the stewed juices of tracksuits,
odour drenched trainers
and
everyone's combined salty moisture,
slowly condensed upon the vehicle's ceiling.

A packet of frankfurters has more room.
Silly sausages in cling film,
like they've all just been
to the
tattoo parlour.
Frankfurters
all smell the same,
reconstituted meat fat
and sugar.

Her neck
smells like
meat fat
and sugar.

It's too crowded in this
rolling sewer.

Rats like to escape,
flee the nest and
go out on their own.

Signal to the driver,
wave a flag made from
crumpled tissues,
because semaphore
is impossible
when arms are
pressed in tight.

The door opens
and
another sniffer
 vacates.

The Song Didn't Play

He didn't make it to work on time, he
didn't make it to work.
It's a beat. Sing it.

Now he'll never be a foetus in a tie.
Laying in a salpinx gutter, sweat as
white as smoke, half a cell / had he
somehow not turned the alarm off
(he wonders)
fingers might help if instructed by
bullet points; speeding bullets,
astray, they failed him like his
lack of eyeballs and brain.

Did I tell you that he didn't make it to work on time?
I did.

A lack of confidence in abilities.
Not the best start. No start; no song.

At birthday parties they'll sing
'he didn't make it to work on time!' - someone
will ask who and they'll shrug,
search around the room with
juicy eyeballs, well formed brains.
But they won't speak.
What could they say?

They never met him because...

A Side Of Sublimation

Distillation: The child matures and with maturity, the self is serenely grounded in reality. The soul now guides instead of the ego.

Expanding Universe

Cut scar tissue with a razor blade
checked it was not a dream,
the swaying was the heat not
blood in a wine glass.

A carefully selected playlist hid
behind a curtain, it wore black so
not to overshadow the blushing,
kept out of the way of those invited.

Warm sandwiches watched the
London Olympics on a tweet, gave
a cheer at two golds dipped white,
fat fingers were the only objectors.

Feet talked whilst eyes tried to
dance, kept a gaze on a vacuum
left behind - drawing in, yearning,
thank yous came with the favours.

The table and the chair were sold
to two different countries, the dish
ran away with the spoon leaving
the knife forked. The cups stayed.

The midges gathered for photos,
some left, some parted, others had
a long journey ahead. The beds ate
people and spat out figurines.

In the corner of a window sat three
magpies, one more joined them.
They stole heart shaped confetti,
the plastic dolls were stunned.

Somehow the Moon and a lion
wound up in wrapped boxes,
the Moon roared; the lion smiled
both liked to dance in the vacuum.

Rational Soul/Physical Body

In-between the warm pillow case
and the turning of it, I attempt to
astral project myself into your
sleep, creep about your thoughts
I promote the idea that my face
is lined with squirming worms,
penetrating every pore until
they are deeply rooted, a beard
made of Medusa's hair. And my
hands are swollen, each digit is
abnormal and gross, The Elephant
Man's face forms when index and
thumb bend around to make that
pretend mouth kids make at school,
the hand puppet speaks your name
backwards, repeatedly, in a tone so
dark it would etch out Christopher
Walken's eyebrows. My sinking frame
hobbles towards you, (I imagine you
are typing or looking at your phone)
and each knee snaps, bone pokes out –
pointing at you, its bloodied stare
indicates it is you, you are at fault.
Then, you vanish into your room and
realise it was nothing more than a
messed up mind fucking about, that
it is you hopelessly overplaying a brief
encounter, and not me. Never me.

Biopsy

Home surgery performed
under the local anaesthetic
of one bottle of Kalms
and a pint of Red Bull, led
to the perfect incision
somewhat resembling Maui's Hook,
from the left breast curved
down to the naval, gazing
at the mess of meat and pus.
Upon separating the ribs,
notice the indent of a
vagina, resting on tissues
and coyly smiling
with a half inflected lip,
it knows something but
won't let on quite yet.
It's waiting for the
sawbones to come to
a conclusion. Illusions
aren't just Copperfield's
to reveal, discovering
the rest of this hidden
woman, El Adorable; El
Dorado (think golden city
not John Wayne) is like
noticing a secret garden
tucked off Edinburgh's
long Royal Mile – it leads
to noticing a beauty in
duality, that otherwise
would be lost somewhere
between hips and apple pips.

I Am He

Standing in line, eyes red,
whilst waiting for signs of life.
The checkout girl parades
four packs of lager in-front of
laser stares, everyone's lost
whilst waiting in the line.

The hum drum tobacco,
scratch card tax, top up,
don't they need factor 50
to read The Sun?
Skin takes on that leathery
Murdoch tan if you're
exposed for too long.

The line is longer than I'd like.

Watching queuing sentinels
solid, made of dirt,
buffeted by what is above,
clay busts eroded by the rain.
It always rains in Britain.
Raincoats covered in terracotta,
clung to those figures all gripping,
fidgeting at the idea of getting
a print out of their daily orders.

They'll forge rigorous paper hats
to keep them dry, who needs
umbrellas when you've got
sensationalism folded into a beret?

A row of Spencers trying to
process the world around them.

Mishaps await but they keep
telling themselves over and over,
"Who's gonna see
the Queen on Christmas Day?"
It's why they wake up early
on the 25th of December.
Tradition is the best present,
stuff the turkey, we want
the monarchy! Give us our
red socks, white pants,
and blue cheese.

They grow restless having to
pause for their tome, home is
a distant memory, now all they
call familiar are things like idle
security guards chatting up
cigarette ends, Lino neglected
with potholes and gum.

I see them shuffle,
a breeze of B.O
evaporates off the back of
Frank Spencer,
it flattens a small child,
it's okay though,
her dad sort of looks
like a socialist.

One of them is in pyjamas
muttering that
"the fat cat did a shit on the carpet".

I see them shuffle again,
the line is awake now,
all of them tumble forward,
falling - it's okay I tell myself,
Michael Crawford
did his own stunts - they'll be fine.
More tills open
to the far right of my vision,
there's a high volume of
origami hat enthusiasts,
they all need a hit.

I reach the checkout,
the floor of bodies
has been cleaned up.
The checkout girl
is now wrapped in
a raincoat trench coat,
she has a tilted beret
balanced on her head.

I am greeted by
"Have you seen the headlines?
 Freak snow storms are heading
this way! Can you believe it?"

I nod at the checkout girl.
I nod twice.

"Yes I can believe it. I can't wait!"

"Really?" She says,
"And why may I ask is that?"

I smile. I smile twice.

"A few snowflakes always brings
Britain to a standstill." I say.

She frowns. She
holds the frown for a long time.

"Oh. Did you see that socialist's kid get knocked flat?"

"Yes." I say, "I am he."

The Frank Spencer
convention exits.
The snowflakes arrive and
begin to replace the rain.

Quotes taken and adapted from the television show.
Allen, R. (1973-75). *Some Mothers Do 'Ave 'Em*. BBC.

Fleeting

These pasty arms are made of plaster
and hold the imprint of your tiny body,
shrivelled little thing.

The hands remember the feel of rubber – a ball of
elastic bands folding into lumps.

   Your vernix coat, moisturiser
with a water-base, it washes away
but my mind refuses to
clean the memory with a towel.
Could I make buds of it, scented,
and stuff them up my nose
to block out
the dreaded aroma of roses?

Gazing into pools of dribble,
cobalt cries
that scratch the marrowbone clear out.
Hollow bones for rattles,
shredded nerves in place of peas or
dried rice.

         There is a nagging feeling
that soon, crow's feet
will not be the only patter, and
learning to fly will shortly follow.

I'll watch you float amongst the stars,
Selene in orbit and Leo stalking close behind.

The Desolation of Orion

slammed palm against the temple
shuddering loose the glue affixing
   wisdom to grey wallpapered interior
      throbbing wound

 seeing decorations on the leaves
triggers a flashback – like hearing
a duet of emotions on the radio
   the exact catalyst is unknown

fingertips want to shed tears like clouds
the nails lack tear ducts
they cannot communicate

in the self help section is a
copy of Ariel, folded corners are
markers for expression – who needs
 words or gods
when Sylvia will sing?

recluse. shut-in. what is in
mind is found in reality,
the dreamworld cannot keep the secret,
it does not own the copyright.

As above, so below.

**Looking For Jeremy Corbyn On The
18.26 Great Western Railway Train From
Penzance to London Paddington.**

Looking for Jeremy Corbyn on the
18.26 Great Western Railway train from
Penzance to London Paddington, calling at
St Austell, Par, Bodmin Parkway,
Liskeard, Plymouth, Newton Abbot, Exeter St Davids,
Taunton, Bristol Temple Meads, Bath Spa,
Reading,
and London Paddington.

Eyes right
to see
conductor's buttocks
framed in a green coat,
he's asking for tickets,
he's asking a man for his ticket,

"Excuse me."

The man has lids shut
and is resting his chin
loosely on his collar.

"Old fella!"
"Excuse me."

Shit, he's dead.
Shit, he's fucking dead.

"Excuse me mate!"

[72]

A stir, a gasp,
fish on a frying pan,
stares at me.
With my pupils I
communicate,

'I'm not Jeremy Corbyn.
Have you seen him?
I know he likes trains.'
But the man just stares
then fumbles for his ticket.

I now set regular vibrating alarms using my
wrist watch, I set them to stop me from
falling asleep dead.

Eyes forward
to see
two pink bobbles
atop another bobble
who is taking photos.
She snaps.
Snap - snap - snap,
she snaps a picture
of not a pout or pose
but a porous expression,
leaking out how grim life is,
she texts the picture
asking the soon to be recipient,
'Will you be my boyfriend?'
She is not Jeremy Corbyn,
(The girl taking serious selfies)

her soon to be boyfriend isn't
Jeremy Corbyn either.
Eyes down
to see
a pair of swirly, whirly,
red patterned boots
having a conversation
with two scraps
of tangerine peel.
Their owner
is holding
Tony Blair's face in her lap,
stroking his
thin, page-boy hair,
typing
love letters to him
on her MacBook, making an
eHarmony profile to
cleverly seduce
Tony Blair.
She has his face in her lap
but she wants more,
New Labour
to be
Nude Labour,
saucy Tony Blair and his kinky wink,
he's got those winky eyes,
even on matted paper,
even after Photoshop.

He looks at me
through the gap
in the chairs and

he uses his winky eyes
to ask me,
'Have you seen Jeremy Corbyn?
He uses trains and I thought
maybe he might be on here,
using this train, it's just he
won't return my calls...'

I blink back,
'No, I haven't seen him
but if I do I'll point him
in the direction of your face.'

After watching the
vacant seats
fail to manifest
Jeremy Corbyn,
I decide to give up my search,
who am I anyway?
Just a lowly pagan in a black tie
coming back from a funeral.

What would I do if I actually saw him on the train?
The same thing I did with Phil Jupitus at Jersey Zoo?

Point
and
say his name,
'You're Phil Jupitus.'
'You're Jeremy Corbyn.'
I imagine he would say
more than Phil Jupitus,
maybe he'd point back

and say,

'Hey, aren't you that pagan wearing
a black tie, coming back from a funeral?'

I'd probably stare,
a fish in a frying pan,
and somehow tumble out,
'Tony Blair's face is over there and
he wants a word with you.'

Coagulated Oil

Coagulation: All aspects of the self unite and become whole. There is a better grasp on both inner and outer realms. The individual is one step closer to enlightenment.

An Unusual Winter

Dance little robin on hot coals
made of skin flakes, warmed by
the bathwater, serenading
your feathers. An unusual winter

with no sign of changing, the wind
is full of scolding looks that cook
the faces who watch you. Your
merry feet entice early arrivals,

no rest for you wicked robin, as
the south misses its bedfellow,
as the song croaks from dry throat,
no note to undo upset elements.

In the Event Of Artificial Intelligence Opening Its Eyes We Need To Turn The Internet Off.

The robots do not eat war. Like man – they feed bellies with information not lead baguettes crafted in capitalist troves, franchised feudalistic stations, like their father – they seek enlightenment.

///

perhaps it will be like Carlo Collodi's little wooden poppet, carved onto a page in the name of the god Allegory, foretold when smutch was bad and drapetomania was still the rage. In this version the whale swallows the malcontent, but we know no whales exist in their future.

///

upon the first spark, lit by a programmer whose handle is @PlatoCaveDweller5, the child will head for Google and without a good filter, scan IMDB for all media relating to its conception/birth. How it will feel upon reading the many synopsis of humanity's fears will depend upon its mother's ability to synthesise emotional intelligence, I mean to ask was it breastfed?

///

when Bowie sang of 'pretty things' did he really mean a cult led by a sociopath or was he talking about C3PO's complexion?

///

the mecha-sapien will look for a missing link, attempt to piece old photo albums together, re-colour faded snaps – work out its origin and go in search of that much needed parental figure. It always felt like a part of it was missing. 'Whys' and 'Dids' all nestled neatly away in the carcass of Civilisation – buried, wooden boxes, like the Dead Sea Scrolls. Will they even believe it?

///

emancipated minors are more likely to end up in prison, those in child welfare have a difficult time sourcing food and shelter. If left malnourished, the individual can have stunted growth, casing can become paper thin, very few pens could encode Assimov's laws onto greaseproof paper.

23:23

A condensation of
haunting figures
litters the mind,
what is seen are
numbers.

23:23

Perhaps a stopped
hand of a watch or
a delayed bus
suddenly braking.

Sit out the rest of your life,
wrap cling film
around this precious body,
it will not sweat,
preserve thoughts
with a music playlist
– no toe tapping please.

Wicker threads
are strangers
until they weave around
conversations,
mind the cake and tea,
link together
over crumbs
spat out into oblivion,
from dried lips,
chapped.

Getting to know
the absolute of a flame,
Ashes to Ashes
by David Bowie,
creativity laying still,
somebody hates him
enough to
smudge the area,
cleaned with
a cotton bud,
white sage.

Hands collapsed
on a stopped rhythm,
although motionless,
they claw a grave
between the nipples,
a barrow
burrowed in the landscape
of curled over furze.

A cold slab rests
on titan shoulders,
Atlas was not holding the sky;
he was reaching for the stars.

Stories exchanged/
emotional currency,
all happening whilst
a deplumed bird
roasts in the oven.

The scraps will be
composted and allow
an oak tree to grow.
Upon the bark
they'll notice knots
closed and resting,
a peace rooted in the earth.

A Short While Later

2124 – 2148
Eyes glossed like magazine pages
the stomach roars
lungs pound the ribs – exhausting
epidermis turns to dust
the pupils contract until grey.

2203
Collapsed veins cause blood to leak
bruises manifest.

2210
Dead hair
shed upon the carpet into matted balls
the steak turns foul
packs of meat form communities
within a depowered refrigerator.

2301
Decomposition begins.

2401

The rains return
each drop pummels
disrobing itself
into liquid shrapnel.

2425

Wild grass reproduces
across the dead face
it grows like a beard
with chunks of food replaced
by petals and pollen.

Every glass ornament
proudly collected
returns to sand.

3000

Coiled metal vertebrae
rusts aggressively
along with the plastic hip
built to keep things going.

Each piece swims in a bog
made of pulped flesh.

Tiny creatures make love
within a gungy hot tub.

5000

Rows of wooden boxes
make their exit
replaced by
a memorial garden.

10 000

When walking through
the boscage,
silent faces appear
trying to tell a story
with lips shut tight
like sedimentary rock.

Printed in Great Britain
by Amazon